CONSCIOUS LEADERSHIP
IN THE WORKPLACE

"*Conscious Leadership in the Workplace* is an excellent guidebook for those leaders who want to lead more effectively and achieve satisfaction in their lives and careers. As Chamberlain astutely points out, when leaders develop a higher level of consciousness and self-awareness, they inspire others and serve as role models for growth. Clear and to the point, the book addresses blocks and behaviors that can impede conscious leadership and provides tools and exercises to increase success and enable reaching one's potential."

—**Bruce D Schneider**, founder, Institute for Professional
Excellence in Coaching (iPEC) and author of *Energy Leadership*

"A topical, practical and hands-on guide for any practitioner of leadership, organizational development, or diversity and inclusion. The expertise with these topics shines in Rosalie's writing, and is highlighted by her passion for the material. A great read for anyone seeking personal or professional growth!"

—**Dave Ruderman**, Management Instructor
University of Colorado Denver Business School

"This is a book where the title truly describes what you will find inside, a leader's guide to be more conscious and aware so that we might make a real difference in the lives of those we lead. Rosalie's approach to mindfulness and self-awareness is direct and candid, and pushes the reader to engage in the process of uncovering our leadership style on a deeper, more personal level. This is a must read for any leader who wants to move beyond the superficial level of 'political correctness' and connect with their direct reports and peers in an authentic way that will positively move an organization forward."

—**Linda Newman** Leadership, Development Consultant

"This is the real stuff. It gives tools to dive into what it takes to become a conscious leader—to become part of the change. Whether you are leading yourself, another or an organization, each chapter will push you toward a new level of leadership. This is for the leader you already are and how to get to the next level. Rosalie challenges us into becoming powerful, caring and honest with ourselves and others in order to create better relationships, work places and ultimately a better world."

—**Cynthia Schwartzberg**, LCSW Integrative
Psychotherapy, Trauma and Empowerment Therapist.

"Rosalie Chamberlain's book looks at leadership in a holistic way. She has created a fresh approach to leadership by bringing issues that show up in a leader's world like fear, diversity, unconscious bias, and authenticity together and to the forefront. A valuable guidebook for everybody who wants to become a conscious leader—in and out of the workplace."

—**Elke Säeubert**, Founder, Xkultur,
Leadership & Cross-Cultural Coaching

"*Conscious Leadership in the Workplace* really packs a punch. The author does a great job of bringing to your attention those things that affect you and your interactions with others of which you are likely unaware. Reading—and using—this book will help you not just in the workplace but in life. I highly recommend this book to those who wish to be more active and deliberate in their decision-making process."

—**Karen Hester**, Executive Director, Center for Legal Inclusiveness

CONSCIOUS
LEADERSHIP
IN THE WORKPLACE

A GUIDEBOOK
To Making a Difference
One Person at a Time

ROSALIE CHAMBERLAIN

New York

CONSCIOUS LEADERSHIP IN THE WORKPLACE
A GUIDEBOOK *To Making a Difference One Person at a Time*

© 2016 **ROSALIE CHAMBERLAIN**.

Published in New York, New York, by Morgan James Publishing. Morgan James and The Entrepreneurial Publisher are trademarks of Morgan James, LLC. www.MorganJamesPublishing.com

The Morgan James Speakers Group can bring authors to your live event. For more information or to book an event visit The Morgan James Speakers Group at www.TheMorganJamesSpeakersGroup.com.

ISBN 978-1-63047-672-4 paperback
ISBN 978-1-63047-673-1 eBook
Library of Congress Control Number:
2015943132

A **free** eBook edition is available
with the purchase of this print book.

CLEARLY PRINT YOUR NAME ABOVE IN UPPER CASE

Instructions to claim your free eBook edition:
1. Download the BitLit app for Android or iOS
2. Write your name in **UPPER CASE** on the line
3. Use the BitLit app to submit a photo
4. Download your eBook to any device

Cover Design:
Rachel Lopez
www.r2cdesign.com

Interior Design by:
Bonnie Bushman
The Whole Caboodle Graphic Design

Interior Graphics:
Jan Marie Lockett, Laura Bean, Victoria Wolf and Bruce D Schneider

Editor:
Alexandra O'Connell
http://alexoconnell.com/

In an effort to support local communities and raise awareness and funds, Morgan James Publishing donates a percentage of all book sales for the life of each book to Habitat for Humanity Peninsula and Greater Williamsburg

Get involved today, visit
www.MorganJamesBuilds.com

Habitat for Humanity®
Peninsula and
Greater Williamsburg
Building Partner

To Jack

You are my amazing support for bringing this book to fruition,
and are committed to living and leading with consciousness

And to Sam and Bolan

Continue living and leading your lives consciously

CONTENTS

ACKNOWLEDGMENTS

This book would not be possible without the incredible love and support of many people. Jack, the idea that developed into a dream began a long time ago and would not have been realized if it had not been for your amazing, constant support and belief in the idea and the message. Thank you, for the multiple reads and re-reads of the versions along the way and your thoughts and suggestions. You have been a strong anchor, guide and reminder to not let the dream fall away or talk myself out of it. And, here it is! Thank you.

Sam and Bolan, you are the greatest gift any mother could ever have and I have learned so much from watching you grow into the talented and caring men you have become. You have no idea how many times along the way, trying to help you grow, I had the opportunity to look at my own preconceived ideas and biases about how things should be. I am grateful to have had the opportunity to challenge my own thinking along the way. May you continue to live joyously, consciously and fully contributing from your authentic selves.

To those wonderful friends and colleagues who enthusiastically supported me through the process. Thank you to those who read through and/or discussed the initial drafts and provided feedback with their thoughts, ideas and questions: Mary, Kathy, Linda, Elke, Al, Hannes, Cynthia, Mary and Tricia. To the wonderful women in my book group, Elisabeth, Elke, Linda, Melissa, Moira, Priscilla and Vicky, where sharing ideas and different perspectives has been a joy and a wonderful experience. Thank you, for your support.

To the many leaders, colleagues, mentors and friends along my journey, who have encouraged me and empowered me— Linda, John, Cathy, Cynthia, Elizabeth, Arin, Cathy, Caren, Bryan, Aimee, Elisabeth, and Ann—thank you, for the support to keep growing, searching and achieving.

Thank you, Bruce and Liz for the incredible work that iPEC (Institute for Professional Excellence in Coaching) does and the permission to incorporate the Energetic Self Perception Chart in this book.

Thank you, Alexandra, my editor. I never knew finding an editor would be as easy as it was. It was because you really "got" me and my message and my style. It has been a pleasure working with you and your skills.

To the many leaders I have known and worked with who are continuing to do the work of developing consciousness and realize that inclusion is a key factor. They know that it empowers a workforce and realize the importance and benefit of having a diverse organization. Keep seeking and striving to create change and empowerment.

I am grateful for that inner guidance that, in the words of Martin Luther King, Jr, guides me on "how to take who I am, what I can do and who I want to be and use it for a purpose greater than myself."

INTRODUCTION

I work with organizations and individuals to help them be more successful. Together, we address their goals, their dreams of developing and improving what they do, and how they can create an environment that supports and promotes the excelling of their workforce. Over the years, I've heard from both current leaders and from individuals within the organization who desire to lead that they want something *more* in their career: something more purposeful, connected and empowering to themselves and others. Sometimes, they can't quite put their finger on what they are looking for. They feel like something is missing but they are not sure what.

I contend that what they may be looking for is work that aligns with who they are and expresses their greatest potential. They want work that is integrated into their lives in a holistic way, rather than separate, ungrounded and unaware. They want to bring more of themselves into what they do, and align their purpose, their passions, and their possibilities.

Bringing ourselves into what we do requires an awareness of self. This sounds like an obvious truism, but this is where many of us can fall short. It could be that we've learned a cultural lesson that work is separate and that our gut feelings, passions, reservations, inhibitions and preferences are also separate. Another possibility is that we've learned to make work impersonal, and as a result, we cut ourselves off from the number one driver of our success and the success of the organizations and the people we lead.

Consciousness is awareness, and awareness starts with our individual self.

Merriam-Webster defines consciousness as "the condition of being conscious; *the normal state of being awake and able to understand what is happening around you*; *a person's mind and thoughts*; knowledge that is shared by a group of people" (emphasis added). In this book, I am going to talk specifically about awareness of self and others. When we are aware, we can know that something (such as a situation, condition or problem) exists; we feel, experience, or notice something by thoughts, sounds, sensations, intuition or emotions. We know and have a better understanding of what is happening in the world or around us. And we are more capable of effective decision-making and leadership.

By now, many of us are familiar with the term Emotional Intelligence (EQ), which is the ability to monitor and recognize our own emotions and the emotions of other people, and to use that information to guide our thinking and behavior.[1] The characteristics of EQ are Self-Awareness, Self-Regulation, Internal Motivation, Empathy and Social Skills. Emotional Intelligence is an essential component of conscious leadership.

Anytime you want to move toward an outcome or goal, whether it is something new or further development of what you are currently doing, you have to know where you are (and what that feels like, e.g., empowered, stuck, certain or uncertain) in order to start and identify the next steps. Chapter 1 introduces the steps for beginning to empower you to identify where you currently are and where you desire to be. Where we currently are is a more important part of the picture than many of us realize, and that is a primary focus of this book. It is about understanding what is really going on, where we want to be and how to get there.

This book is about consciousness as it relates to the individual, and more specifically, how leaders can understand the impact of consciousness and the importance of further developing a deeper awareness. We are going to look at what that entails, and how you can transform leadership in the workplace and in your life. We all lead, whether we are leading others in organizations, in our communities, associations, or in our individual lives.

I have done a significant amount of work with organizations and individuals on diversity and inclusion, and when I wanted to write a book that would further the discussion and contribute to making a difference, I knew that transformation really is a one person at a time

1   See Daniel Goleman's foundational book, *Emotional Intelligence*.

task. An organization can check the box on a number of diversity and inclusion initiatives and programs and include the importance of diversity in its mission, and it can do quite well; however, until each individual is aware of how they impact the business, themselves and others, real change that is sustainable will continue to be a very slow process. Conscious leaders play a huge role in organizations, and can act as catalysts for growth. Conscious leaders are naturally inclusive and as a result, the organization benefits from the utilization of the rich and varied talents of the workforce. But each leader must do the work themselves to become more inclusive; leadership starts with you.

Because of the idea that each individual is so important to creating environments that are successful, high-performing and inclusive, this book is a guidebook for making a difference—one person at a time. We start with ourselves first. If we continue to address the ways we interact with our teams and with the world at large, we can become a model for others who seek to achieve their own goals. Together we will go over simple steps for bringing greater consciousness into your leadership. This book will look deeper into what being inclusive means, talk about the differences between misconceptions and reality, and what gets in the way of becoming an empowering and engaging leader working with an energized, productive team.

A word here about developing greater consciousness. It can be simple, but it is not always easy to achieve and sustain. It takes intent, commitment and practice. Consciousness is part of a lifelong journey that requires focus and awareness all the time. It is not an "oh, I've done that and now I've got it" type of exercise. Each person who wants change must set their intention to delve into who they are, how they show up, and why they desire transformation, if anything is going to occur. That's why this book is for those who want more. It is for those who want to *know* more deeply and access their whole self. Not everyone may be interested in this type of transformation or feel they are ready to address it, and that's fine. Those who do, agree with the business leaders and individuals I meet who want that something more than what they have right now. If this is you, then congratulations! You have taken a first step and are motivated for change. I hope that this book will inspire and guide you.

—Rosalie Chamberlain
Denver, Colorado

Note: For illustration purposes, this book includes some examples of situations which are real. Names have been changed to maintain the privacy of the individuals.

CHAPTER 1

WHO ARE YOU
AND WHAT IS THE MESSAGE
YOU ARE BROADCASTING?

If your actions inspire others to dream more, learn more, do more and become more, you are a leader.
—John Quincy Adams

Leadership

In some form, we are all leaders. Whether we lead others or lead ourselves; whether it is in our work environment, our community or personal life, leadership goes beyond a job title. We can own this state of being, all the time.

We tend not to think this way as a general rule. Most of the time, we defer to external criteria to define leadership. These criteria can include a position in a company or in the community; a checklist of technical objectives; or a group of people being led. We often see leaders as presidents and executives, people with specific industry or skill qualifications, degrees or certificates. We might consider ourselves leaders if we manage a team of people, either at work, in a volunteer position, or within our families. These are external criteria: leadership has been conferred on us or others through outside means.

Is that what leadership really is? An outside-directed force, a category we can be placed into? There is something significant missing from this model of leadership, and what is missing is "us."

What about internal criteria? What qualities does a conscious leader have? Here are a few that I see in my work with individuals who successfully lead:

- Appreciative of diversity
- Accessible / Approachable
- Beliefs are congruent with actions
- Clear
- Collaborative
- Compassionate
- Continual learners
- Courageous
- Curious
- Dependable
- Emotionally intelligent
- Empowering
- Focused
- Grateful
- Have integrity
- Have positive energy
- Honest
- Humility
- Inclusive
- Intuitive
- Intentional
- Learn from unintended outcomes

- Motivated
- Motivating
- Non-judgmental
- Open-minded
- Purposeful
- Self-aware
- Visionaries
- Willing to be vulnerable

Notice that these characteristics are things which leaders *are*, not what they *do*.

Forbes put together a list as well. In 2012, they published their top 10 leadership qualities.[2] These include honesty, an ability to delegate, communication skills, a sense of humor, confidence, commitment, a positive attitude, creativity (in decision-making), intuition, and an ability to inspire others.

All of us can learn to embody these internal qualities. All of us can learn to become thoughtful, conscious leaders.

Broadcasting and Self-Awareness

As individuals we have an innate need and desire to grow, to continually better ourselves. In the business world and in our personal lives we have a desire to develop and to be successful. Let's explore the idea that consciousness and leadership begin at the individual level. After all, every team, every family, every organization is made up of individuals. Higher levels of success and achievement begin when each and every person takes responsibility for their own growth.

If I take ownership and responsibility for my own growth, that means I need to ask myself:

2   Tanye Prive. "Top 10 Qualities that Make a Great Leader." *Forbes*.

- Am I clear about what I want and are my actions congruent with my values and goals?
- Do I learn from every outcome, whether I planned for it or not?
- What is my intention and do I communicate it well, and am I moving forward with intent and commitment?
- Do I understand the impact of my intention and actions?

These questions bring us to the heart of the process of conscious leadership, and creating success for ourselves and others: the process of self-awareness.

> **Leadership and learning are indispensable to each other.**
> —John Fitzgerald Kennedy

Here's the deal: whether or not you are aware of the answers to these questions yourself, those around you are aware of *you*; we broadcast this information about ourselves every day. The quality of our leadership shows up in the messages we broadcast. It is imperative that we know ourselves.

One leader I know, Robert believes that effective leadership cannot be an on-the-surface type. What does this mean? I interpret this to mean that the leader and the organization cannot put forth a type of window dressing, the kind of "front" that gets someone in the door; but then, the actual quality of the merchandise or leadership, such as meaningful work, accessibility, development and approachability are not what was advertised. "You have to say what you mean and mean what you say." And here, it goes both ways. Whether you are a leader in the organization or the new employee looking for the best place to grow and develop your career - say what you mean and mean what you say. It is a commitment on each party's part.

How do we find out what we broadcast, and whether we are disseminating what is best for us, for our success and the success of others? Several chapters in this book will come back to this key point: We learn what we broadcast when we stop and take a look at ourselves.

Consciousness is *paying attention*. Most of us have something we want to achieve, at work, at play, at home, in ourselves, or in our communities. We need to pay attention to find out what that is exactly, and how to get there. We cannot know where we want to go or who we want to be if we do not know who we *are* first. For this reason, this book will involve a lot of self-examination. This may be a less than comfortable process for some, but will reap powerful benefits.

In my business of helping organizations become more inclusive with the diversity of their workforce and helping individuals have success in their lives and careers, I am convinced that individual responsibility and consciousness are at the root of getting the life, career and organization you want. Nobody else can do this for us, just each one of us taking responsibility for ourselves and our actions. The common thread is, how do you show up? The following questions will help you gain a better understanding of yourself and where you are now in the process of your leadership:

- Who *are* you?
- What do you have to offer?
- What holds you back?
- How do you contribute to the constructive movement for change and how do you block it?

If we as individuals let go of our fears about self and others, shifts occur and inclusion can take place. Organizations will attract and retain employees that are diverse and multi-talented and individuals will shine and exhibit peak performance. *We* are often the number one obstacle in the path to our own goals.

Leadership comes with the responsibility of self-awareness. Not only must we be aware of our team and our organization's purpose, but we must also be aware of how we share what we *do* and how we *are* to the world around us. When leaders are in their consciousness and giving freely, they are inspiring others and serving as role models for growth. The signal is: I am here, I am present, let's work together toward excellence. Conscious leaders are willing to be vulnerable (more on that later) and step back, evaluate and adjust or clarify when their message does not get across; because their ultimate goal is to create, engage and collaborate. It is difficult for a team to disengage from a leader who is present in this capacity. What is being broadcast enables honest response. When leaders are defensive and afraid, their teams can be defensive and fearful as well.

Individuals within organizations have to navigate corporate culture and often take their cues from the individuals around them. Effective leaders have to lead and set the tone for that culture and that team. Both have to take charge and determine how to do this. It is an *individual* responsibility. Each of us needs to see where we are living up to our values and where we are sabotaging our achievement to reach our goals. Instead of looking around, let's look inside.

Now, if living a more conscious and authentic life is not something you are intent on focusing on at this time, this book may not be for you. Yet you picked it up; something drew you to do so. Perhaps you feel you are not achieving the levels of success that are possible. Perhaps you've tried other avenues to achieve your goals and found them unsatisfactory or incomplete. Perhaps you are merely curious. In working through these pages, you may discover something about yourself, who you want to be and who you really are and how you can take steps toward greater leadership.

In my experience, conscious awareness is a powerful catalyst for change, and for success. Don't worry, if we do not have a strong sense of conscious awareness, we can create it. That is what this book is about. How do I get where I want to go? What steps can I take that will effect real change? I want to reiterate that the journey into creating consciousness, while it may seem simple, is not always easy to do. If undertaken honestly, this journey may, in fact, be a challenging process. The rewards, though, are generous. Zen practice has a saying, "Every step of the journey is the journey." Each step along the way provides immense growth and peace if pursued with diligence and intention.

===== **Exercise** =====

It is helpful to discover, define and write down our goals and desired outcomes with respect to becoming self-aware. These can form your roadmap toward success and you can add to or take away from it from time to time. The important thing is that you begin to see what it is *you* really want.

1. Recognize who and where you are in the present.
2. Do you give the best toward the common goal? If not, why?
3. What price are you willing to pay to achieve your desired goal?

On a scale of 1-10, rate yourself with regard to your level of commitment to give your best. If you are not at a 10, what would it take to move up the scale? What is one action you can take to move forward in that direction?

CHAPTER 2

THE ELEMENT OF FEAR

I'm not afraid of storms, for I'm learning how to sail my ship.
—Louisa May Alcott

Why Talk About Fear?

Once we've taken a look at where we *are* and where we desire to be, we want to consider one element that could be keeping us from moving forward: Fear.

Fear is not something we like to focus on because it contributes to making us feel fearful. Ironically, we are then avoiding the most effective way that exists to diminish our fears. Research into courage has found that acting courageously requires an understanding of our anxieties; denial does not support action.[3]

I offer that the element of fear can enter into anyone's life in some aspect at any time. Sometimes fear shows up as feeling vulnerable. Sometimes it shows up as uncertainty and anxiety when you do not know how to do something well. However it shows up, it is still fear.

Some people like to think of themselves as fearless and many people appear to be, especially when it comes to certain capabilities, skills and talents. Just look at the athletes who compete in the extreme sports categories. However, many of us will have something that trips us up sometimes.

Some fears are larger than others. Some are more conscious to us than others (we will explore the unconscious in greater depth in Chapter 3). Discovering what the fear is as well as the cause and repetition of its message is an important part of self-awareness. This particular topic will also be addressed in several chapters of this book because that is how fear works. It shows up in various times, places and elements of life.

Part of the journey of transformation and development is to understand what your fears are and how you can transform them into success. The choice to let vulnerability hold you back, or to help you move through your fears, is yours. If you choose to let it hold you back, remember it is *your* choice. There may be a sense that this is okay; you have been okay with it for a long time and you are quite

---

3   Carolyn Gregoire. "The Science of Conquering Your Fears—and Living a More Courageous Life." *The Huffington Post*.

successful. You may even enjoy where you are as there are secondary gains and pleasures that may feel satisfying on the surface, but there is frequently an underlying dissatisfaction once you are committed to building your awareness and consciousness. When this happens, you realize on some very important level that this state of being may not serve you toward achieving what you desire. You will enjoy a much more fulfilling and authentic life if you risk moving through the vulnerability. Your leadership will also benefit.

An important distinction: When I speak of fear, I am not talking about fear based on experiences of blatant abuse of or by another person. Many people have had horrific experiences in their lives in which their persons, their emotions and/or their intellect, or property were brutally attacked. There could be a long road to healing in such circumstances that may require the help of a psychiatrist, psychotherapist and/or doctor. When I talk about fear in this book, I am talking about a conditioned response to a non-life threatening trigger.

Vulnerability can show up as fear. If you are deepening your self-awareness and working on skills to make you a more conscious leader, accept that you will feel vulnerable at times. Franklin D. Roosevelt's famous quote is relevant in working through the feelings of vulnerability.

> **The only thing we have
> to fear is fear itself.**
> **—Franklin D. Roosevelt**

Sometimes there is fear of what we think, and this is self-defeating. For instance, one of my clients was struggling with a constant voice that told her that she had to have a certain level of health and fitness or she was a failure. In our coaching sessions, we looked at the old familiar "voice," where it came from and how she had for the most part "ingested" it so that it became her *overriding voice*. The recurring thoughts about her health and fitness were very stressful for her because they subtly showed up at times when she was focusing on her leadership. We utilized a number of strategies including awareness and some Neuro-Linguistic Programming (NLP) techniques around beliefs. One of her discoveries was that she was *afraid of the actual thought* she was continually having because it was not consistent or congruent with who she was as a leader. On some level she was very clear that she was often quite successful as a leader, but the little voice in her head that questioned her success in other areas of her life was constant. It took her off her focus and made her question herself. This was very enlightening. This fear of *what we think* shows up more often than we are aware of. We do not particularly like to admit we have fear or that we could succumb to the fear. It is important to explore this type of fear when we are committed to looking at our biases and judgments, which we will explore more in the following chapter.

I am a fan of Brené Brown's books and TED talk on vulnerability.[4] I especially like how she asks us to show up. The people around you

---

4   Brené Brown, PhD is a research professor at the University of
     Houston Graduate College of Social Work. Her 2010 TED

will respond to your openness, and this gives you the opportunity to exercise true leadership. Is a guarded, disguised fear truly what we wish to broadcast?

Influencing Factors

Many influences contribute to a feeling of fear. These can include our environment, experiences, background, structures, teachings, cultures, personality, and behavior—the list goes on. Some of these influences are external and some internal, but whatever the contributing factor is, F.E.A.R.© can cause us to come to a screeching halt. What happens when we experience F.E.A.R.©?

F – We are in *Fight* **or** *Flight* mode; we become defended and often defensive.

E – We *Exclude*; we can become isolated and separated from others and even ourselves.

A – We *Avoid*; we avoid seeing other perspectives or looking deeper into cause and effect.

R – We *React*; we react from our emotions, sometimes focusing on the past or a perceived future.

Houston talk on the power of vulnerability is one of the most watched talks on TED.com, with over 15 million views. She is the author of *Daring Greatly: How the Courage to Be Vulnerable Transforms the Way We Live, Love, Parent, and Lead*, among other books.

© Rosalie Chamberlain 2015

Image 2.1. The cycle of F.E.A.R.© perpetuates a
negative feedback loop and blocks our awareness.

The diagram in Image 2.1 shows the vicious cycle that fear
creates. Staying with fear keeps us in a feedback loop of emotional
reactions driven by fight or flight responses, which lead us to exclude
and avoid people or situations we find challenging. In turn, our
exclusion and avoidance fuel more fear and misplaced reactions. We
can step outside of this feedback loop and transform the direction
of our thoughts and actions by becoming aware of our fears and the
reactions they set off in us.

Consciousness of what causes our F.E.A.R.© has to take place individually. No one can do the hard work for us, and we can't do the work for anyone else. Each of us needs to come to a deeper understanding of how and what we do, and how we contribute to situations based on our actions, thoughts and behavior. This takes courage.

Transforming Fear

As we mentioned previously in Chapter 1, the bottom line is we need to know who and where we are and identify where we want to go. Revisit the goals and desired outcomes you thought about while reading Chapter 1. When there are decisions to be made, challenges to be dealt with, uncertainty, and we begin to recognize that F.E.A.R.© is present, it is helpful to start asking questions about each of the components of F.E.A.R.©:

F – Who and why do I want to **fight or flight**; how am I defended and what am I defending against?

E – Who am I **excluding** and how am I isolating and separating from others and from myself?

A – What are my beliefs and perceptions and what other ways of viewing a situation or person am I **avoiding**?

R – What are my emotional **reactions** and where are they coming from within my experience?

Fear can express itself as a sense of doubt about something or someone, or as self-doubt, uncertainty, or insecurity. Fear may jump in when you least expect it. It may also jump in when and because you *do* expect it. We often get what we think about and believe may happen. To the extent you can, put these fearful feelings on the shelf and focus on the action you want to take. Avoid allowing fears to "talk" you out of acting with clarity and courage. Facing fear head on does not mean you never hear the voice or feel the feeling again, it just means you respond differently, with a confidence connected to knowing what lies within you. You see the fear for what it is—a sign that you are leaving your comfort zone. When you are aware of your reactions and put your fear aside, your confidence has the opportunity to flow naturally.

When fear is not faced, questioned and transformed, you run the risk of creating a vicious cycle that perpetuates the fear. It will continue to show up in circumstances that are *not* true fight or flight situations, but you cannot see past the immediate feeling because your reactions are automatic and often unconscious. Bring the fear into consciousness—this is your next step toward becoming a conscious leader.

Exercise

Think of a time when you were successful in moving through fear because you were confident in your abilities in that situation. Then, uncertainty or fear began tugging at you because the situation may have become more challenging or more of a risk. Remember how you moved right through the fear because your confidence and certainty kicked in.

1. How did you step outside the F.E.A.R.© cycle?
2. What questions did you ask yourself? Or, what statements did you tell yourself?
3. What conclusions did you reach that allowed you to move forward?
4. What awareness from that situation that helped you through the challenge can be available for future challenges?

CHAPTER 3

THE UNCONSCIOUS AND UNDERSTANDING BIAS

To know the true reality of yourself, you must be aware not only of your conscious thoughts, but also of your unconscious prejudices, bias and habits.

—Anonymous

Introducing the Unconscious

The unconscious is a vast topic—just as our unconscious mind is vast. It stores our experiences, memories, events, teachings, thoughts, and perspectives. It stores our fears, as previously touched on in Chapter 2, and it stores our unconscious biases and habits. As we grow in self-awareness, we would be well served to dig into the information wielded by our unconscious mind.

When I speak of unconscious bias, I mean beliefs, judgments and automatic thought processes that are unknown, submerged, hidden from view. They are outside of our awareness. Our goal in becoming self-aware is to shine a light to bring these unconscious beliefs and processes to the surface, into our conscious awareness.

The unconscious does not discriminate as to the validity or appropriateness of the information it takes in, and it takes in everything. It does not know, or care, if the information is true or false, real or unreal. Over time, much of this information gets reinforced. The messages about ourselves, others, situations and experiences become the beliefs by which we operate. These messages are the mental shortcuts in our brains to make some sort of meaning or create a sense of understanding of our world.

Because there is simply so much there, we need to be intentional and methodical with our deeper dive, taking one small piece at a time. We are going to focus first on our unconscious biases. In later chapters, we will look at our triggers, dualistic thinking, and the way our ego operates. Even in persons with very high Emotional Intelligence (EQ), if there is a lack of awareness of one's unconscious bias, this can impact the person's ability to consciously lead and provide an environment of inclusion where everyone can succeed.

Understanding Bias

Bias lives in both the conscious and the unconscious. Self-examination of unconscious or implicit (hidden) bias can prove to be uncomfortable as it can often conflict with our conscious beliefs.

This is very important to grasp and hopefully diminishes some of the discomfort about exploring unconscious bias. Consciously, we may want to be inclusive; unconsciously, we may be afraid of perceived outcomes. There is often resistance to talking about bias because we fear discovering what we think and feeling that we are "bad" for having bias. When we come up against an unconscious bias that is at odds with what we consciously believe, we often jump to value judgments about ourselves, such as: I must be horrible for thinking that!

Bias is part of the human condition. We are not "bad" for having bias. We can have bias for, or against, something or someone. Remember that we are dealing with an automatic shortcut, a reaction our minds have created. The often-unconscious original intent may have been to make our lives easier or safer. We can now bring awareness into the equation and dismantle shortcuts that no longer serve. Biases that are unconscious can significantly impact our decision-making and outcomes. We need to become aware of what they are, and how they impact ourselves and others, so that we can achieve our noble intent. It is critical to know what our biases are because they can be the precursor to stereotyping, prejudice, discrimination and various types of "isms" such as racism, sexism and classism.

Here is an example of an unconscious bias conflicting with a belief that Susan revealed to me in a conversation after a program on diversity, inclusion and bias. She worked with someone on a matter and was very pleased with the interaction and with the outcome. She told me that she had only worked with him in a professional setting, thus they were usually dressed in either business casual attire or in suits. Then, one day she saw him at a kids' sports game. Both were there with their children and it was a warm afternoon. Susan noticed that the business associate had multiple tattoos on his arms. Susan said she had to struggle with that fact because she discovered she had an unconscious bias about people with tattoos that told her, "*They* are not professional." Yet, she consciously knew from experience that he was very professional and she enjoyed working with him.

It is important to bring awareness to your unconscious biases. When an unconscious bias causes you to decide that you will have little or nothing in common with someone based on a preconceived judgment, you can miss out on possibilities for fruitful interaction or building a meaningful relationship. This is not an uncommon phenomenon.

Multiple Types of Bias

There are many types of bias that are not necessarily recognized or thought of as such. We often think of bias as it relates to race, gender, sexual orientation, age, physical and mental abilities, religion, ethnicity and/or cultural background. Consider the following as a fraction of a list that reflects various other aspects of diversity:

- Communication style
- Language/Accent
- Veteran status
- Socioeconomic status
- Geographic location

- Political affiliation
- Thinking style
- Personality
- Education
- Family status
- Work style
- Organizational level
- Experience

Bias can show up in relation to any of these and then some. Look back at the list. What topics resonate with you? What instant message or association have you automatically assigned to that aspect of diversity? The task is to be aware and notice how your thought process drives your behavior.

You can Google "bias" and find many terms and descriptions, some more subtle than others, that in the past may not have been thought of as bias. Part of the work around understanding unconscious biases is recognizing that they can be very subtle and taken for granted. This leads to a perception that how you see things is "just the way it is" and believe that therefore your perspective is, or should be, the same for everyone. My friend and colleague Dr. Arin Reeves discusses some of the subtle biases in her book, *The Next IQ: The Next Level of Intelligence for 21st Century Leaders.*

Harvard psychologist Mahzarin Banaji and University of Washington social psychologist Tony Greenwald have done a significant amount of work on blind spots and hidden biases. They, along with Brian Nosek of the University of Virginia, founded Project Implicit®, a research collaboration. Project Implicit "investigates thoughts and feelings that occur outside of conscious awareness or conscious control." The Implicit Association Test, found at https://implicit.harvard.edu/implicit/, is an interesting exercise in measuring hidden associations. Project Implicit is an ongoing research study. The research seeks to identify a distinction between our explicit and implicit bias.

To what extent do our biases, without our awareness or conscious control, shape our likes and dislikes, our judgments about people's character, abilities, and potential? This is important information for anyone in leadership. Conscious leaders are committed to becoming aware of their biases and exploring their impact on decision-making, inclusion, strategy and development. As much as possible, we want conscious intentions to guide our decisions. As we become aware of our unconscious biases, we can take steps to align our behavior with these conscious intentions.

Bias is a part of and shows up in life and, hence, we often bring it into the workplace. Careful study can reveal that it may be present with regard to gaps in leadership and specifically with respect to diversity of gender, people of color and individuals who self-identify as lesbian, gay, bisexual and transgender (LGBT). Beliefs are not always easy to transcend. It warrants a close and focused awareness of biases when setting policies and procedures and strategies that will be implemented for an entire workforce.

This also applies to development programs, succession planning, business development and advancement. If you are responsible for setting policies and procedures and communicating internally in your organization as well as externally, you will especially benefit from a dispassionate look at the source of the decisions you make to determine if potential bias contributes to the decisions. We want conscious choices to be the foundation of our practices.

In your organization, it is important to be mindful of the diversity of your workforce and understanding there may be gaps in leadership with respect to women and minorities. The critical thing is to make decisions based on qualities and the expertise needed for a position. That being said, one has to know if the company is recruiting from a diverse pool; if they are providing equal opportunities to all of their employees; and whether they are making their choices based on facts and not assumptions, biases, judgments and stereotypes.

In working with organizations on gender diversity, I have seen some high potential women hold themselves back because there is a perceived stigmatization that they may be derisively defined as "aggressive," while a man in a similar position in the organization is described as "assertive." A conscious leader would set a cultural tone and atmosphere that encourages everyone to bring their full voice to the table. I had the privilege of working with a leader who not only always encouraged me to give my opinion, but exhibited genuine interest in what I had to say. He valued my opinion, even when we did not see eye-to-eye.

This raises the point that bias about others and the way we perceive they are or will be works both ways. Recognition of bias is not just the leaders' responsibility. For instance, if you are biased about a leader and determine it is not in your best interest to give your opinion because of fear of how you will be judged or that you will not be heard, or that you will fall under some stereotyped image, you may be missing opportunities to contribute which may also escalate the success of your career.

Once you have begun discovering your hidden biases, assumptions and stereotypes, you will also begin to notice where you prejudge people and situations. This is very important because prejudging impacts everyone involved. If you are a leader and you are prejudging a person, the ability to discover their uniqueness and potential contribution can be significantly impacted. So is your ability to be inclusive. How can you really "see" someone if you have already decided how they will be? What might you be missing? Again, it is about awareness. Listen to the internal talk. What does it say?

Further Discovery and Examination

There are numerous authors and articles on hidden bias, unconscious bias and implicit bias. I recommend further study for discovering the way bias shows up in your life and delving deeper into your own ability to identify and explore your biases. The References and Resources sections of this book can provide a few places to start. I invite you to explore further on your journey of self-discovery.[5]

Here are some guidelines to recognize internal dialogue that can show up as "red flags" that assumptions, biases and stereotypes may be present:

- Would I say the same about another group?
- Do I think "All," "Every," "They" about a specific group?
- Do I rationalize, thinking "*this person*" is an exception?
- Do I base my evaluations on someone's actual behavior or am I evaluating only on my opinions, judgments and assumptions?
- Do I make assumptions based on look, voice, appearances?
- Where/how did I learn my assumptions, biases, and stereotypes (from friends, family, media, personal experience)?
- If I had a one-time personal experience that was negative with a member of a particular group, do I expect or believe that all future experiences with this group will be negative?

---

5   See Merida L. Johns, PhD, RHIA. "Breaking the Glass Ceiling: Structural, Cultural, and Organizational Barriers Preventing Women from Achieving Senior and Executive Positions." *Perspectives in Health Information Management*; Judith Warner. "Fact Sheet: The Women's Leadership Gap, Women's Leadership by the Numbers" *Center for American Progress*; Catalyst. *Narrowing the Fortune 100 Gender Leadership Gap: Change is Closer Than You Think.*

Be careful that you do not halt the exploration because you are judging yourself harshly as you go through this process of discovering your biases. It is about discovery. Rethinking old messages can be difficult when there is self-judgment. It is important and effective to have a mindset of curiosity when delving into our unconscious thoughts. Being aware of how your biases impact your decisions and behaviors will make you a better leader.

A Change is Coming About

For a long time, the discussion of bias was somewhat taboo and I had clients who preferred not to include this discussion in my diversity and inclusion programs. It was okay if I mentioned bias, but that was sufficient and a deeper discussion or presentation was not to be on the agenda at that time. The tide is changing. I now have calls specifically for consulting and programs on understanding bias, both from current and prospective clients. Often, they want to take the discussion deeper and gain greater insight into how it shows up in their organization and in themselves. One compelling force creating change and developing interest is the fact that there is disparity in gender, racial and LGBT diversity in leadership, and if an organization truly wants to be an employer of choice and a great place to work, attracting top talent, it is imperative to implement a deeper look at practices and procedures. It requires examining how bias shows up in the hiring, review, evaluation, development, advancement, and retention processes.

Another propelling force that has set in motion a strong desire to explore bias is the recent number of reports in the news on incidents involving racial tensions. These worst-case events inspire a need to develop stronger awareness and explore these issues. When tragic incidents involving race happen, discussion can often become a debate. People begin taking sides. I offer you this suggestion as you hear or read about reports such as these: look at your reaction. Do you automatically take sides, believing or disbelieving all that you read or heard or saw? I suggest this not to bring about a decision as to who is right and who is wrong, but rather to stop to see if you are perpetuating a particular stereotype, bias or racism.

While some of this momentum for change has come from concern about large scale national and international occurrences, as well as from organizational goals to become more diverse and inclusive, continued change also applies to you, the individual. On a day-to-day basis it is important to bring awareness to your reactions and thoughts and how they impact your community and world view. When you begin to bring your own unconscious biases to the surface and notice a preconceived judgment, not thought out thoroughly, or that came from a learned experience or someone else's opinion, what do you do with it? Do you agree, accept it as truth and move on as usual? If this is the case, what can be the impact of this small, seemingly normal action? It can be huge.

If you are a leader and you accept someone else's judgment of a person without careful thought, experience or facts rather than opinions, this can have a tremendous impact on that person's career. If you are someone who is building and leading your career and you accept another's opinion about a leader or the organization that sets off a tendency in you to hold back and not excel because of a comment or feeling perceived as disempowering, watch out for this. If it threatens to stifle your motivation, think it through! You would be well served to not let your performance excellence be squashed by another's experience or belief. Take charge of your career and explore your own biases.

One leader, George, told me that one of the greatest Ah Ha moments he has had was understanding the hidden nature of unconscious bias and that once he began to explore and welcome the insight, he began to see how subtle and deceptively hidden it was. He noticed that underneath his conscious awareness, there would be an event that brought about an image, followed by an immediate reaction, and that his subsequent actions were influenced or impacted based on that habitual response. He shared that he looks at focusing on his conscious thought, examining it, and thus making choices as to the behavior and actions he wants to implement.

Addressing Bias

Addressing bias is not always easy, but a key point is to have communication. This cannot happen without taking the risk to develop understanding through listening and sharing thoughts and perspectives. I was recently asked how to respond to comments that are offensive. The mother of a young woman who was engaged to a man from another culture and race was asked if she was concerned about them marrying, stating that it must be hard to deal with. The mother was shocked and stunned at what she felt was a racist comment. She did not say anything at the time but she really wished she had. It is not always easy to think on the spot and say what could be more helpful. The purpose in exposing bias is to understand, educate and change our behavior from judgment and exclusion to inclusion. My suggestion to her, should a similar situation arise, was that she could respond with a question, such as "what do you mean?" or "what do you think will be hard?" This gives the opportunity for a dialogue to take place and for new perspectives to occur.

Contributing to change by transforming old messages and teachings is powerful. I grew up in the 50s and 60s, and I was given many messages of prejudice, stereotypes, sexism, racism and bias about differences. By questioning these messages, I found that deep inside, the discomfort I felt with these old teachings disturbed me and they were not congruent with what I believed. This moved me to work toward unraveling, disputing and transforming my life and my career. Going through a self-discovery process that reveals exclusion of and misconceptions about others is empowering. It has empowered me to strive to live more consciously every day in all that I do.

======== **Exercise** ========

Begin to notice where you have judgment, fear and withholding in a situation or around some individuals. Notice judgments that pop into your head and what the messages are.

1. What assumptions are you making?
2. How might you be stereotyping an individual into a particular group?
3. Explore the early messages that influenced your perception about the particular topic.
4. What was the message and how did it impact you?
5. Are you resistant to certain subjects or aspects of diversity and inclusion? What are they?
6. Where did they come from?
7. How true are the assumptions and judgments you made? How can you influence change in future circumstances by being aware of your bias and actions?

Experiment: Establish a Judgment Journal and note in the journal the judgments you make about others and about yourself, and see how fast it fills up.

CHAPTER 4

KNOW YOUR TRIGGERS

The amygdala in the emotional center sees and hears everything that occurs to us instantaneously and is the trigger point for the fight or flight response.

—Daniel Goleman

The Brain

The amygdala is one of the deepest, oldest (in terms of evolutionary biology) parts of the human brain. It performs a primary role in the processing of memory, decision-making, and emotional reactions, and therefore plays a huge role in our internal feedback loop of fear and unconscious bias. This is the emotional center of the brain, which processes everything that occurs to us and is the trigger point for the fight or flight response. The feedback loop from the trigger to the reaction is blind and happens instantaneously. It is a "shortcut" from trigger or stimulus to reaction or response.

The amygdala is not involved in higher-order cognitive processing. Executive functions, such as planning and strategizing, organizing, and paying attention to and remembering details, are handled elsewhere in the brain. If we let the emotional responses of the amygdala have their way, we are shortchanging our abilities as leaders. But how do we influence a process that happens so quickly? As with the other steps in our journey towards becoming conscious leaders, we need to start by developing *awareness* about what triggers set us off (*or push our buttons*), and the emotions they release in us.

How it Works

Let's start with our old "friend," Fear. Behind many assumptions, biases and stereotypes lies fear. It is a powerful trigger, and also great at disguises. It is sneaky and convincing at rationalizing the reasons for thoughts and actions.

For example, you may think that taking on a certain task is not something that you are particularly adept at, even if it is something you would really like to accomplish. What are the reasons you think this way? It may be that there is a subtle uncertainty that is weighted with a feeling of vulnerability or fear of a negative outcome that holds you back. Notice if there is a sense that it is out of your comfort zone. If that is the case, then you can definitely choose to stay with the status quo. However, you may also have a pretty good idea that it would be something that would benefit you and others in the long run. Your rationalization may be that it is just too much to take on right now. While the timing of taking on something unfamiliar may be a real factor, the tendency could be to dismiss the opportunity and not revisit it again. That may be a valid decision or it could be a missed opportunity. And, if on some level, you know that it is something you would really like to do and it could benefit the organization, another approach would be to determine if there is a strategy that could assist you in moving forward with the task. Then, identify any resources you need. This can happen if you are aware of the discomfort and perceived vulnerability. You can then choose to act from a clear and knowledgeable frame of mind rather than rationalizing away something that is important.

This type of reasoning is worth examining on a deeper level. Beliefs we have (often erroneous) beneath the discomfort and sense of vulnerability can be self-fulfilling. Conversely, when a limiting belief is challenged and a different and empowering belief is taken on, that too, can be self-fulfilling. Just take a few minutes to think back on a time when you wished you had done something and you did not. What was the message or rationale you applied in making your choice? What if you had chosen differently; what might the outcome have been? If you determine that you would likely proceed differently in the future for a similar situation, it could be helpful to be aware of limiting beliefs and take actions that can then move you forward rather than rationalizing or "talking yourself out of it."

Another way rationalizing decisions triggered by fear may manifest is when a leader chooses to work with the same person all of the time because he or she is sure of that person's work and work product. This can be understandable on one level because we enjoy working and are comfortable with people that we have experience with and a similarity to. However, when there are others on the team who could also contribute different talents, skills and perspectives but do not have the opportunity to do so, there is the risk of low morale, discontent and feeling undervalued and disrespected. In the long run, not only do you run the risk of developing other team members at a different rate than the person who is always chosen, there can also be retention issues with those whose talents are underutilized. Other organizations are looking for top talent, too.

So, if there is an underlying level of fear and uncertainty that keeps you as a leader from getting to know the full strengths of your workforce and utilizing and developing that talent, begin to examine the "truth" behind your rationale. What is the potential impact on your workforce, the individual and the organization? Not only is there a risk of not retaining top talent that you need, there is also a risk of impacting the ability to attract new talent if the word-on-the-street is the organization is not a place where everyone can have the opportunity to grow and succeed. This is very important to consider: that you may be missing diverse talent and skills that can produce powerful outcomes.

In both cases, the individual who does not want to step outside their personal comfort zone, and the leader who prefers to work with one individual or group because of predictable work rather than challenging and growing the rest of the team, the rationale to hold back may appear reasonable and justified on the surface. Underneath that surface, however, may lie the true motivation: there is fear of the discomfort or the difficulty that choosing to act otherwise could create.

As noted previously, fear that underlies bias about others can show up both ways. It can show up in the individual who wants to succeed but holds themselves back because of fear, and it can show up in the leader who cannot see the talent that is right before them because there is too much focus on what/who is comfortable. The sense of discomfort or difficulty and our emotional reaction to that discomfort is the trigger process we are looking for.

Identifying Triggers

Triggers show up in our emotional reactions. They do not always look like fear, though I believe a kind of subtle fear is at the root of each one of our triggers. If we have done some work on our unconscious biases, it may be helpful to review what we've discovered. Protecting ourselves from fearful situations is only natural. Our built-in desire for safety comes from a long ago evolutionary time when human beings had to be defended and reactive against the real dangers to their physical existence. There was no time to ponder. For survival, the reactions needed to occur instantaneously without lengthy thought. However, these days our fight or flight instinct is overused and overworked and not always in proportion to its natural, instinctual purpose to protect us from truly harmful situations. We do experience—or our brains interpret experiences as—threats to our sense of well-being, to our sense of self, to our sense of success. Whether perceived or real, this "threat" brings on the same reactions. In order to become more thoughtful leaders, we need to grow in awareness of the difference between real bodily harm and perceived personal threats of a less existential kind.

Triggers are important to be aware of because triggers and fears become habits. The more we allow them to operate below our full conscious awareness, the less power we have to change them or to create a different outcome based on more beneficial insights and habits. Just as with our unconscious biases, triggers can cause us to miss valuable opportunities. If we are triggered to react emotionally to our colleagues and team members, we may overlook the ways we can support each other's success. We have a choice to proceed differently, but often don't recognize it (more on choices in Chapter 5). Our realities will become (or remain) governed by these triggers.

David had a habit of not really listening to his team's contributions even though he "appeared" to listen. He began to question why some of the members in his department never spoke up and was initially drawn to question if he had the right people in place on the team. In reality he knew he had hired a diverse group of smart and talented people, so he began to consider what he might be doing as a leader that had an impact on the innovation of the team. It took a lot of courage to be willing to look deeply at his own behavior. He realized that when others were providing

A powerful partner in the way our thoughts create our realities is language. Begin to listen to language—yours and the language of others. Notice if you use words like "hate," "don't like," "crazy busy," etc. My clients are amazed at how their energy and perspective shifts when they recognize language that has a negative tone. Our words help create our reality and empowering words have an amazing impact on that reality. You can generate positive changes in yourself and in others simply by paying attention to the words you use.

Words can trigger negativity. Probably many of you have had the experience of reacting emotionally to what someone else has said. What words trigger your hot buttons? What do others say and do that trip your emotional trigger? In order to grow in conscious awareness, we have to know what our triggers are and be aware of what happens to us when a trigger occurs. The next time one of your triggers is tripped, explore the following questions:

- What is happening to my energy?
- Where is my focus?
- What can I do to get back on track, get grounded or centered?
- What motivates me and what de-motivates me?

For instance, if you get off track on a goal or action because something did not go quite the way you anticipated it would; do you give up, beat yourself up, complain about the situation or the others involved, and create a vicious cycle that keeps you running on a hamster wheel? Our reaction to triggers happens instantaneously. As you work more deeply on your awareness about triggers and their effects, remember to take a breath and slow down. By slowing down and learning about the trigger and your defensive emotional reaction, you have a better chance of ending these types of internal struggles. You benefit, and so do those you lead.

Exercise

1. Identify a challenge you see and experience in your world.
2. What are the perspectives that are learned and the ones that are habitual? List these.
3. List alternative perspectives to approach the perceived challenge. Once you examine other perspectives, what might be another way of looking at the challenge or situation?

CHAPTER 5

DUALITY

Nothing is either good or bad but thinking makes it so.
—William Shakespeare

Duality and the Box

Duality presents another challenge to effective leadership. Dualistic thinking assumes a universe where there are only two contrasting, mutually exclusive choices or realities. This thinking is either/or, bad/good, negative/positive and has a powerful effect on our belief system and actions.

Dualistic thinking contributes to our fear by presuming the false restriction that no other choices exist. When we think this way, we are locked in, with little freedom. We may feel stuck in a situation, or as though we lack a sense of independence. Our opportunities, our choices and our willpower may seem stifled. We tend to react emotionally in such circumstances, sometimes not even aware of the reasons why. Dualistic thinking is a powerful trigger for our fear pattern of behavior.

Many of us practice dualistic thinking on a daily basis. We evaluate the situations and people around us—and our own thoughts and feelings—on a binary scale. We often don't allow for a spectrum of possibilities, and this is the primary way dualistic thinking becomes a roadblock in our personal and professional growth. By identifying only two choices, we close off our ability to see other paths forward.

Think about the various experts in business advice and personal fulfillment. How often are we advised by such people to "think outside the box?" Dualistic thinking is the perfect "box." Instead of considering multiple ways we can succeed or ways our business and career can prosper, we are bouncing back and forth between the walls of our box.

If we believe that something is good or bad, we have assigned a judgment based on our experience, learning or habits. As with any bias, we are prejudging. Instead of evaluating each experience on its own merits, we evaluate situations or people based on the category our judgment places them in. Think about all the insights we lose when we do this! It is staggering.

There is a danger for us in dualistic thinking that hampers learning to become more conscious leaders beyond that potential loss of insight and information, and missed opportunities discussed

Fear of differing perspectives is an interesting phenomenon. When you are in fear and duality, you really do not want to hear, and I mean *really* hear, another's perspective. There could be a misconception that taking in another perspective to understand where someone is coming from will invalidate your own perspective. *Either* your perspective, *or* mine. This is a dualistic way of thinking. Nothing could be further from the truth. Your unhealthy ego (see more in Chapter 6) is getting in your way.

Dualistic thinking encourages us to get territorial about our points of view. However, our work environments demand that we be more collaborative than ever before. An inability to negotiate multiple possibilities is a serious barrier to our own personal career and can present obstacles to creating collaborative teams. On a personal level, we can wreak all sorts of damage to interpersonal relationships by maintaining this dualistic approach.

How to Transform Dualistic Thinking

Be aware if you are only paying lip service to wanting to hear multiple perspectives at the table. Recognize how often you really consider these perspectives and even set your own perspective aside to determine if there may be another way to enhance the outcome the team is trying to achieve. Be curious about how you react to alternatives beyond your own. Just as I am asking you to not prejudge situations with dualistic thinking, also do not prejudge yourself. Recognize that your triggers and unconscious biases have likely been playing a leading role in your thought processes up until this time.

This type of recognition of the part your triggers and biases play in your behavioral and decision making process takes practice; we often need to be aware of these dynamics more than once to learn what we need to move forward.

Keep in mind that considering other perspectives is healthy and it is more than putting yourself in another's shoes or frame of mind. It is about examining what happens to you in your own shoes when you are faced with people, ideas or situations which are different and that make you feel uncomfortable, threatened, insignificant or insecure. Can you think of any reasons why you might feel resistance to this process?

There may be consequences or results that come with whatever decision you make. Sometimes those consequences may seem like a choice between what you leave behind versus what you gain, or there may be things that you enjoy with either choice. An important thing is to realize that it is often unrealistic to think that there will not be feelings about our choices. Thinking one choice is "right" only when everything is lined up perfectly or in a way you determine is perfect is limiting. Once you realize this, you can focus on what seems to be the best course of action for the situation. Stepping away from the idea that only one choice is "right" frees you to see what may be most helpful and useful in a variety of options.

When we are not operating from a dualistic mindset, we can experience non-attachment to an outcome and invite and entertain possibilities and perspectives that have a powerful impact.

Duality blocks our progress. The more we can break through this either/or mentality, the sooner we are on our way to nurturing greater consciousness and success, in the workplace and in our lives.

Exercise

1. Listen to your either/or thinking.
    a. How do you recognize duality at work in your thoughts?
2. Listen for the one versus the other thinking.
    a. Notice if there is tension, anxiety or resistance to other perspectives and suggestions.
    b. Explore why this might be.
    c. Do you fear or believe in a negative outcome as a result of a different perspective or suggestion?
    d. Allow yourself to consider a neutral possibility.
3. Take the process deeper by discovering if there is a fear or belief of a negative outcome if your preferred way is not chosen.
4. Explore a middle ground.
    a. What if it is neither good nor bad, and it is just different—different from your usual way of being or doing?
5. While observing your either/or thinking, be aware if you are focusing on having a dialogue or a debate.
    a. In dialogue, you are interested in what the other has to say and they are interested in what you have to say. In a

debate, it is a clear intention of either/or, right/wrong—that focuses on win/lose.

b. How often do you have a dialogue, and how often do you have a debate?

c. Can you think of a situation where dialogue would be the most useful type of communication?

CHAPTER 6

LEAVE THE EGO AT THE DOOR

I work really hard at trying to see the big picture and not getting stuck in ego. I believe we're all put on this planet for a purpose, and we all have a different purpose... When you connect with that love and that compassion, that's when everything unfolds.
—Ellen DeGeneres

Healthy and Unhealthy Ego

In the previous chapter on duality, I briefly touched on a concept referred to as the "unhealthy" or "little" ego. Many of us are familiar with the term "ego" being used to describe the sense of self that we have, a self that is separate from other people. This is often how the study of psychology uses the term. I'd like to posit that the ego can be either healthy or unhealthy: a sense of self that serves us or one that does not.

The healthy ego is that which motivates us to develop and be authentic, and, for me, to be aligned with my whole self—mind, body and spirit. The healthy ego is interested in further development and is able to understand and overcome fears that are not empowering to us, instead of holding us back from being our best. A healthy ego moves us forward and connects our intuition and healthy sense of self. Our healthy ego allows a high level of self-esteem. When we have a healthy ego, we understand that the way to measure self-esteem is to measure it within ourselves. Self-esteem is not about you being compared against or above another.

A healthy ego, as you might guess, requires self-awareness.

How can we judge the health of our egos? When there is a feeling of openness to others' perspectives, ways, similarities and differences, our egos are more likely in a healthy state. We realize that other perspectives exist beyond our own, and don't feel threatened by them.

The unhealthy ego or little ego, by contrast, is often ruled by fear. It is limiting and is likely dualistic. The little ego measures you against others or situations and its make-up can contain negativity, unhealthy competition and victimhood. The unhealthy ego wants more than anything to be comfortable and safe, and seeks always to create a comfort zone around itself, setting up barriers to different perspectives or others. The trouble with this is that the comfort zone is an illusion; if we were truly comfortable, we wouldn't need barriers.

There are many apparently successful people who sometimes operate from unhealthy egos. That is, we call them successful because of their title, their income, their power or the developments of their company. A clue for us to evaluate this apparent success is to explore the culture such people create around themselves. Do their colleagues enjoy their leadership? Do the individuals within the organization feel valued and empowered to contribute? Is there a high level of turnover at the organization? Is the environment healthy for everyone?

Comparisons

As mentioned above, the unhealthy ego is focused on comparing self to others and not necessarily in a productive way. Over the years, I've often thought that comparisons are disrespectful. A good friend commented to me when my second son was born that she thought comparisons are odious. She said it in relation to her children and I took it on in relation to mine. As a parent, one of the joys was being able to see my sons grow and develop into their unique, individual selves. They are not inverted images of each other. In business, when you compare one person to another who you think is a top performer, it is important to look at what unique qualities you may be missing if your evaluation is based only on the comparison of traits you see in the one with whom you are most familiar. Further, it is disrespectful to skip over the uniqueness one can bring to the organization when you only consider the value of what they can contribute in relation to someone else. It is reasonable and wise to have an expectations criteria in place, and at the same time it is valuable to look at each individual with a fresh perspective. It is also important to not have a "one time out" rule in place, meaning that if someone does not meet the expectation the first time around, they should be afforded constructive feedback and an opportunity to have a second chance.

Likewise, keep comparison in perspective in relation to yourself and your work and with respect to those competitive thoughts that slip in seemingly so innocently. These types of comparative thoughts can be a huge contributor toward separating from others and from oneself. What can happen in a situation where the little ego is triggered when comparing itself to others is that it is afraid of not being enough and thus unconsciously believes it needs to be superior. This is a time to explore why we compare. Here comes that fear thing again.

The little ego separates. It separates us from one another for many reasons. It is human nature for us to gravitate toward people like ourselves, so it can be natural to sometimes separate from those *not* like us. As discussed in Chapter 3 on the unconscious and understanding bias, we tend to separate because doing so makes us feel "safe," and it is familiar. Very few of us, if we are completely honest, are so self-assured and comfortable all of the time with every aspect of who we are that we don't "justify" some of the little things we don't like about ourselves. This can show up by pumping up our ego and finding fault with others.

This type of thinking is often based on habits and beliefs that we have held for a long time. True openness to new possibilities, perspectives and outcomes includes having awareness of what those beliefs are, and how they impact us, others and situations. Your healthy ego is not involved in this mindset. You may want to consider setting aside a worry state of "what about me" in the process of becoming a conscious leader. Sound scary? Only to the little ego.

When we work in leadership, we necessarily work in company with other people. One of my favorite sayings is the Japanese proverb, "None of us is as smart as all of us." Logically, we can see that when every member of a team has the opportunity to contribute their talent to the whole team and the entire organization, there is an elevated potential for greater success. The unhealthy ego can stand in the way of this success. It demands attention, and wants the attention all for itself. The little ego is not nearly as smart, talented, or informed as the sum of the whole group it purports to be a part of and to lead.

In business there will be core competencies that are baseline measurements for performance. These are the criteria for success and they are necessary for establishing goals and developing individuals. But sometimes, the comparisons stop here and an individual is defined only in relation to those competencies. When this happens, the unique gifts of the individual may not be discovered and considered. Limiting comparisons such as these do not help define a performance plan or start a conversation that contributes to an individual's ability to enhance their natural talent and skills within the work environment. When judgment occurs that imposes a limiting comparison on someone, it can throw them into the vicious cycle driven by insecurity and fear, which can sabotage performance (see image 6.1). Improvement, real improvement, contribution and awareness cannot happen while in this state. True awareness comes from bringing these unconscious beliefs into conscious awareness.

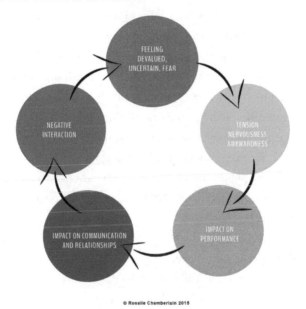

© Rosalie Chamberlain 2015

Image 6.1. Vicious Cycle in an atmosphere of fear and insecurity.

Robert's leadership style is consistent with a belief that not every person or situation requires the same approach or strategy. You have to consciously understand and then decide the best way to lead. You have to know and understand the individual. His leadership style is not "off-the-shelf"—it is not "Leadership 101."

I venture to say you would not be reading this book if your healthy ego didn't want more conscious awareness, connection and personal development to be a part of who you are and how you show up. You are interested in how to be a more effective leader that promotes awareness, engagement and performance excellence.

Healthy egos are not frightened of competition, because they feel a sense of empowerment to continually improve. Healthy egos love opportunities to do great work, to shine and connect with those leadership qualities we covered in Chapter 1 (e.g., learning, non-judgmental, focused, honest, creative and committed). In the process of writing and publishing this book, I have been asked about the title and premise of the book. After explaining the premise, I would sometimes get a response of, "I know some leaders who need to read this book." I received a different reaction from leaders who are diligently working toward becoming more effective leaders, as well as from those who aspire to lead or lead their own careers. Their response was, "I want to read your book." What this says and supports is that conscious leaders are continually learning, which is motivated by the healthy ego. One more thing about egos, healthy and unhealthy: We have both. It is our choice which one will be in charge.

Tools and Exercises

A helpful tool for measuring how well you lead and where your energy is, is the Energetic Self Perception Chart developed by Bruce D Schneider, the founder of iPEC (Institute for Professional Excellence in Coaching; see image 6.2 for the chart). The Energetic

Self Perception Chart shows seven levels of energy, along with the core thoughts, emotions and actions associated with each of the seven levels. These levels help you understand how you are approaching life and leadership, as described in *Energy Leadership: Transforming Your Workplace and Your Life from the Core*, by Bruce D Schneider. As an iPEC certified coach, I often utilize iPEC's modality for growth and change in leadership and life because it resonates with my values and what I have learned about leadership through working with companies and individuals. The further we get from the little ego, which lives in the realm of "self" on the chart, the more leadership qualities come into our orbit. We create more as we move into healthy ego space.

Many of my clients and I also work with their results from taking the Energy Leadership Index™ Assessment, which measures how effectively one leads. The assessment holds up mirrors to our perceptions, attitudes, behaviors, and overall leadership capabilities. We often work with the Energy Leadership™ Development System, which is a great tool for working to develop powerful leadership skills and abilities.

All of these tools and exercises focus on creating a greater level of self-awareness. The outcomes are descriptive, not predictive. You may feel uncomfortable thinking or talking through the insights that come up for you, or acknowledging that you might share thoughts or feelings that are perceived as negative. You may feel vulnerable and defensive. Remember that this is part of the process of developing a more conscious leadership. This sense of vulnerability is a flare-up of the little ego that wants to remain where it thinks it is safe.

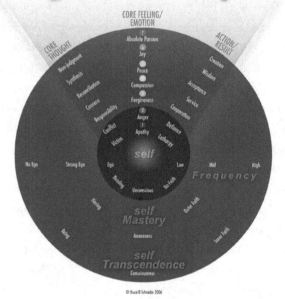

Image 6.2. iPEC Energetic Self Perception Chart.[6]

6   The Energetic Self Perception Chart is wholly owned and used by
     permission of Bruce D Schneider and The Institute for Professional
     Excellence in Coaching (iPEC), copyright © Bruce D Schneider, 1999,
     2006, 2015.

Resist the feeling you may have to protect yourself from change. When you are in the mode of feeling you have to protect, you cannot be open to the ultimate potential that you are and what you can give. What you want to create is covered up by a multitude of thoughts, fears and beliefs.

> **Because of its phantom nature, and despite elaborate defense mechanisms, the ego is very vulnerable and insecure, and it sees itself as constantly under threat. This, by the way, is the case even if the ego is outwardly very confident.**
>
> **—Eckhart Tolle**

The best step we can take for ourselves in this situation is to draw a deep breath, step forward, and leave the ego at the door.

Exercise

Take another look at the Energetic Self Perception Chart developed by Bruce D Schneider. Which level best describes how you see the world? To find out exactly how your energy is distributed among the seven levels, you can deepen the exercise by arranging to take the Energy Leadership™ Assessment to focus on shifting your consciousness and increasing your awareness, energy and leadership capabilities. Contact information for the assessment is found in the About the Author section at the back of this book.

CHAPTER 7

STOP THE BLAME GAME

Let us not seek the Republican answer or the Democratic answer,
but the right answer. Let us not seek to fix the blame for the past.
Let us accept our own responsibility for the future.

—John F. Kennedy

Blame Game

Conscious leaders are not caught up with blaming others for the outcome of a situation. They take responsibility for their own actions and they do not make others wrong. Conscious leaders have stopped playing the blame game.

Now that you have looked deeper into fear, bias, duality, healthy ego behaviors and unhealthy ego behaviors, let's look at how some of

Shifting Out of Blame

What are you defending against? What is the trigger that is prompting you to look to someone or something else as an escape from responsibility or an agent for action? As you unravel these thoughts, you will begin to see how your actions came from your belief about the situation or person, and you can choose to shift and try something different.

Beliefs can be limiting and have the voice that says "not good enough," "not good at," "they'll never accept my opinion," etc. Behaviors can be anything that block you and stop you in your tracks, such as fear, blame, withholding, etc. You can discover new possibilities when you examine your beliefs and behaviors that potentially block you from achieving what you want to achieve (see Image 7.1).

Shifting a belief can feel scary, because the result or outcome is unknown. I know that feeling. I've found that shifting is easier when I approach my belief with curiosity, tinged with a bit of excitement. I remind myself that I am discovering a new way or opportunity. I can see possibility, let go of the daunting feeling of fear, and I am empowered to do something purposeful, that aligns with my deepest desire to contribute, utilize my gifts and talents and add value.

The funny thing is, feeling valued really comes from within. I don't want to discount the value we feel when we make a contribution that takes us out of our box, and others recognize and appreciate what we have done. This does indeed play an important role in whether we feel valued in an organization or group. For this reason, conscious leaders are appreciative and acknowledge the contributions of their team.

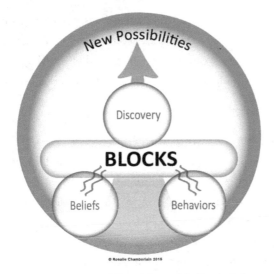

© Rosalie Chamberlain 2015

Image 7.1. The 3 Bs of Growth©. Our beliefs
and behaviors can block our discovery.

What I want to emphasize though, is that this external appreciation can never replace the sense of satisfaction we have by acting on our purpose, our passions and our possibilities. If you do not step into your inner sense of value, you will stay in the illusion that your success and wellbeing are dependent on someone else, and this impacts your ability to make change. When we don't value ourselves, we are prone to slip into blame—a blame that really starts with ourselves: self-judgment.

Letting go of self-judgment is important, and it takes practice. First you have to notice and recognize when and how often it happens.

Just naming it is a step; however, that does not really create lasting change. If there is a common judgment that continues to appear, it will need more work (the exercise at the end of this chapter addresses the issue of self-judgment). Another tool you can use for this purpose is meditation.

Tools and Meditation

Meditation is a powerful tool on many levels, and I recommend it as a daily practice for anyone. Studies have shown that meditation positively impacts health, creativity, behavior and wellbeing. There are many forms of meditation. It is an individual practice that when done regularly, brings about transformation and a peaceful sense of self. After years of practicing meditation, I find that I can access that deep inner guide, peace and creativity in pretty much any situation. It does not require a special position or isolated quiet. I find that I can meditate in a crowd any time of day.

Years ago, I did an intensive self-development retreat. After researching venues, one of which was a very spiritual and quiet place, far from any hustle and bustle, and one which offered me an opportunity to do the retreat in a very busy place—namely, New York City. I chose New York. The retreat was an incredible experience and it allowed me to be able to access my deepest inner thoughts in the middle of one of the busiest cities in the world. I went away from the retreat experience with an incredible sense of renewal, self-knowledge, growth and inner peace and direction. I also figured that if I could do that in the midst of New York City, I could access that part of me anywhere. You can as well.

We already mentioned that self-esteem is a measurement in relation to yourself, where you are, and a celebration of your successes along the way. These are chunks of esteem that you build on. If you find you are struggling with accepting an inner sense of value, try on the belief that there is no such thing as failure. What you've called failure is just an opportunity to learn from actions that did not turn out the way you wanted them to or imagined or hoped they would. You can explore what was limiting and what was empowering. In this mindset, you can determine what you could do differently next time. Stepping away from dualistic thinking and blame gives you options and opportunities for growth and success. The blame game serves the unhealthy ego. It does not serve you.

In my work with individuals and organizations, I often suggest having a Judgment Journal. I encourage them to notice how many times in one day they make judgments about themselves and others, and to notice how quickly it will fill up, as well as how many journals they would use up in a week, if they kept going. I offered you this suggestion as part of the exercise in Chapter 3. An interesting thing about judgments is that they come from our tendency to generalize, delete or distort information. Another interesting thing about judging others is that behind the judgment is often a judgment of ourselves, which is often unconscious or at least pushed aside because we don't want to deal with it (refer back to Chapter 3 and the unconscious).

CHAPTER 8

CLAIM YOUR AUTHENTIC POWER

The truth is: Belonging starts with self-acceptance. Your level of belonging, in fact, can never be greater than your level of self-acceptance, because believing that you're enough is what gives you the courage to be authentic, vulnerable and imperfect.

—Brené Brown

Holding Back

What are the beliefs and behaviors that hold you back?

By now, you've had the opportunity to explore how your fears and your little ego may be preventing you from achieving your next success. "Great," you may be thinking, "I've done all of this self-discovery, and now what?" Some of what you discovered may have been uncomfortable. Now we want to use our knowledge to step into success, which means ownership, responsibility and power.

This book has been brewing, being written in my head and some of the text on paper for about nine years. I initially felt inspired and empowered to make a difference, and then all the voices that wanted to keep me safe, keep me "perfect," reared their heads. They sounded a lot like, "you do not have anything new to say, no one will want to read it, it will be insignificant, it is just your opinion," and so on. I listened to those voices until I decided it hurt more to keep avoiding writing than putting it out there.

> **And the day came when the risk to remain tight in a bud was more painful than the risk it took to blossom.**
>
> **—Anaïs Nin**

You have a choice. I did. We all have a choice how we will view the world and ourselves. The key, as I've said from the beginning of this book, is to know where we are now, where want to be, and what holds us back. I realized in the end that the most important thing about the book is that I wrote it. I stepped out of my so-called, perceived comfort zone and completed the dream I had to write a book about my passion for developing consciousness as an important ingredient for life and organizations. And it felt great!

I claimed my authentic power. I saw where I was, where I wanted to go (write a book), and what was holding me back—Fear—and I knew I could get from where I was to where I wanted to go. That's power. Too often we think of power as one person's influence *over others*. Really, once we have aligned our passions with our purpose, enormous possibilities open up. When we've become congruent with who we are and what we want, *that* is power. One person's influence—over themselves.

Safety Zones

Consciousness, remember, moves one person at a time.

When you have the feeling that you need to stay safely in your comfort zone, realize that safety may not be so safe in the long run. Measuring missed opportunities and "what ifs" is a tricky business. Let us stick with facts. You are reading this book because you are ready to make changes—you want "something more." Can you achieve that something more by staying on the course you have been following? Staying the course when you are really discontent is the tangible risk that likes to pose as safety.

> **Avoiding danger is no safer in the long run than outright exposure. The fearful are caught as often as the bold.**
>
> **—Helen Keller**

Much of our decisions to hold ourselves back, not interact with others, not speak up and share creative ideas are because we have an illusion that holding back will keep us safe. There is certainly a time for discernment, for choosing what is worth pushing ourselves for so we can step out of our box to try something new and/or different. The key to seeing the difference between the two is to know what our *intent* is behind the action. While intent does not necessarily equal impact, the clearer we are with respect to what our intention is—why we want to take the action—the better chance we have of making a difference. We need to recognize real opportunities when they present themselves.

Furthermore, in the long run, staying or playing it safe is *not* safe because there will ultimately be an incongruence with who you are and what you can and want to accomplish, along with the behaviors that we use to keep ourselves feeling "safe." This incongruence or misalignment slowly eats away at creativity; you can become complacent and disengaged. This is not safe. This state of mind is corrosive to your team and your own success. Playing "safe" can be denigrating and over time create a dissatisfaction with yourself and others.

Changing Limiting Beliefs and Stress

Changing limiting beliefs is fundamental to growth. Yet change is more than coming up with a new statement of what to believe, or just trying on a new belief and hoping it sticks. Real change is finding a new belief that is empowering and is in alignment with who you are and your values.

Whether the issue is personal or one related to business, freeing up anxious energy and limiting beliefs with a new way of being is life-changing and allows us to live in our full potential. Sometimes considering what we think of ourselves or others is the sticky spot, that when moved through can lead to great work and transformation. When we free ourselves of anxieties, we can claim our authentic power.

A related issue is stress. Merriam-Webster defines stress as "a state of mental tension and worry caused by problems in your life, work; something that causes strong feelings of worry or anxiety." Clearly, a state of mental tension is a block to claiming our authentic power. Stress is a topic that gets a lot of attention because it can be physically unhealthy. While there are techniques to help manage stress published frequently, I want to look at stress as a wake-up call. Stress can be transformational by building a tremendous amount of awareness of what is going on in our lives and work, and what we can do to change things. Furthermore, conscious leaders understand that stress can impact performance, behavior and mood. Stress affects us personally, and that effect trickles down to the rest of our team.

Stress can be a tool for self-awareness and developing conscious leadership. Remember how we used F.E.A.R.© as a red flag that helps us take a closer look at areas we may want to address? We can use stress the same way.

Stress shows up in the body in different ways for different people. You may feel it as a tension in your neck or back, sweaty palms, tight throat or a knot in your stomach. When this happens, it is time to notice what is happening and why. Here are a few common stressful situations, along with some steps to delve a little deeper into what might be going on with regard to the anxiety you are feeling.

Interacting with stress

Explore your resources. When you have multiple projects and requests and a feeling of too much to do, prioritize what's most important. What resources do you have and what resources do you need to assist you with the process? It is ok to say no to projects and requests, or at least to say that you will be able to get to it on a particular date. Also, notice what is wasting your time and energy. If you are spending time on things that are not a priority and procrastinating on the things that are, find out why. Do you need more resources? Do you need assistance?

Effectively interact with curiosity. Have you ever avoided interacting with someone because you believe you don't have anything in common with them? Having commonality can be a driver or, rather, a drive-away factor, when entering into conversation. Focusing on where you think you don't have commonality will deepen the discomfort. Try being curious about the other person and discover where there may be commonality, even if it is only the fact that you both work in the same organization.

Look resistance in the face. Resistance usually follows fear. You might not like to admit the fact that you have fear and prefer to say you just don't want to do something. That may be the case, but when the task is necessary and you just don't want to do it, what are the assumptions, beliefs or concerns that keep you from moving forward? Fear can be subtle and checking in to see the underlying message can be transformational. Sometimes messages are old but continue to repeat themselves in our unconscious, bringing uneasiness and frustration to our consciousness. What is the old message? Is it still true? What may be a new way to approach or view the matter?

Visualization is a powerful tool. You can create powerful outcomes for goals you want to achieve. We addressed this briefly at the end of Chapter 7, when trying to move from blame to success. One method is to get centered, as though you are going to meditate, by getting comfortable and focusing on your breathing. This can be done sitting up, lying down, or mindfully walking with focus. I like to feel my feet firmly grounded as though roots are extending through the bottom of my feet into the earth. Choose the outcome you want to visualize and bring it into focus as though you are watching a movie. See yourself in that scene exactly as you would like it to be. Feel what it will be like when you have this outcome. Let yourself feel the joy, contentment, exuberance or sense of satisfaction. You can even "hear" what would be going on around you when you have achieved the outcome you desire. Make this a regular habit. This technique can be used for little projects or major changes. It has worked for me in several instances—one of which was when I transformed chronic pain into being virtually pain free.

Set an intention and make a commitment. Setting an intention is more powerful than defining a goal. Goals are necessary to achieve things you want (and even those things you are not that engaged in doing). Accomplishing those goals is easier when you set an intention. When we are intent on doing something, the energy behind our action is stronger. Once we've set an intention, and we make a commitment, we put things in motion. A commitment is where the rubber meets the road: when we commit, we are focusing on that intention and that drives us toward the goal. The commitment is the action that is going to begin to move you forward. Making a commitment is powerful when you really want to do something. When you are aligned with what you intend to do, it does not feel like work. Instead of a negative stressor, intentions and commitment are motivators that create rather than drain energy.

Use stress as another tool for self-discovery. The more you know, the more you can step into your authentic power. This is the firm foundation on which you can develop your leadership and build your success. Notice also that the wake-up call is really a call for self-care—a time to look at what is going on and why; and what you can do to mitigate the stress by making conscious choices.

Exercise

An important aspect of claiming your authenticity is fully assessing what is important and how well you are aligned with your whole self. The following questions and exercises are important tools for creating alignment.

1. Write down your values, as many as you feel are important to you. Then narrow the list to the top five things. Where does each value currently show up in your day-to-day life? If there are any that sit in the shadows that you would like to bring more front and center, which one(s)? Why is it not a primary contributor? How can it be made into a primary contributor?

2. On a scale of 1-10, one being lowest and ten being the highest, how integrated are your mind, body and spirit? Now, spirit can mean various things to different people. It is not necessarily religious, as it can be intuition, wisdom, higher self, divine—however you define it for you. There will be times when we utilize one aspect more than another, and at the same time, the other two are still a part of who we are. What does the integration of your mind, body and spirit look or feel like for you? Begin to notice these three aspects and how they interrelate in your day-to-day activities. Ignoring one or more parts can ultimately lead to imbalance. The Aristotle quote, "*The whole is greater than the sum of its parts*," can be a guiding statement to maintaining a balance of mind, body and spirit.

3. Consider a meditative practice as a regular part of your daily life. Whether it is a walk outside, a calm quiet time set aside, reading something that is empowering and motivating—it does not matter. Just focus on whatever gives you that sense of being calm and connected, free of worry or fear, and fully

present. Find ways to make this an important part of your life—just like eating and sleeping and brushing your teeth. After a while, you will be compelled to do it. There are many books on meditative and mindful practices. A couple I recommend are *Search Inside Yourself: The Unexpected Path to Achieving Success, Happiness (and World Peace)*, by Chade-Meng Tan, and *Mindfulness: An Eight-Week Plan for Finding Peace in a Frantic World*, by Mark Williams and Danny Penman.

4. What gives you joy? What energizes you? How much of that energizing factor do you have in your life and work? How can you have more?

5. If you were to give a TED Talk, what message would you give? Once you have determined your message, assess whether it is a part of how you show up in your work and in your life.

6. What "stories" have you invested in about yourself? How have they worked for you? Do they align with your values? If not, how would you rewrite your story to be authentically you?

CHAPTER 9

CONFIDENTLY LEAD
YOURSELF AND OTHERS

*We gain strength, and courage, and confidence by each experience
in which we really stop to look fear in the face... we must do that
which we think we cannot.*

—Eleanor Roosevelt

Leadership Happens

Leadership happens everywhere—in our homes, families,
communities, work, country and the world. We have a choice to lead
effectively, or not.

We have covered a lot of ground in the preceding chapters about
recognizing the characteristics of conscious leaders. We have touched
on the types of things that get in the way of being conscious, and how

to recognize when we step into a pattern that may not serve us or our leadership. What has hopefully become clear is that the characteristics of conscious leaders are individual characteristics, and we each have to work on our own leadership individually.

Discovering our passions, our purpose and our possibilities are the top resources we have for leading in our own lives, and for leading others. Taking action on just about any matter is much easier when you can align the actions with your passion and your purpose and desired outcomes. I predict you will have a strong sense of gratitude for being able to move away from seeing the learning opportunities as "struggles" and instead seeing them as possibilities.

Your Values

At the core of conscious and effective leadership is awareness: self-awareness above all. This book has given you some questions to explore, which you can pass through once on this reading, or revisit as often as you like or need. They are a way to drill down and help you discover what it is that you truly value.

It is imperative that you learn to understand what you value and how it plays into your leadership. Approach this question with a sense of curiosity. Once you know what you value—and do not judge it—you cannot *not* do what you are called to do and what you have passion for.

I am thinking of one successful leader, Brenda, who valued perfection. When we began working together, her emphasis on perfection felt like a barrier to what she and others wanted to achieve together. Rather than trying to eliminate the value she placed on perfection, she learned to adjust her past behavior; instead of remaining someone who was never satisfied, she became someone who valued the essence of what motivates her from a healthy ego place: she valued the desire to continually improve.

Once you "know" your values, they can serve as an effective guide. As a leader, when you realize that what you value is a driving force for being better at what you do or envision, those values can be assets for you, important ingredients in what you want to accomplish. You can tap into your values not from an obsessive place, but rather from a creative and appreciative space. When you can see the impact of your values in yourself and others, the experience that it brings out is very different.

We broadcast our intentions and values every day, whether or not we are aware that we are doing this. We are more successful in work and life when we *are* aware of our patterns, our fears, biases, triggers and unhealthy ego choices. We can lead from a position of strength; "knowledge is power," as the saying goes.

Conscious Leader Characteristics

In the opening chapter, we looked at some characteristics that conscious leaders share. What does this look like in practice?

Conscious leaders are at peace with themselves. They are free from complaining because they see opportunity in all situations. They are slow to anger and can manage their behavior. As a result, they give their team and their colleagues the chance to also see opportunities, and the space to bring up creative solutions.

Conscious leaders are not thrown off by criticism, as they know that this is another opportunity for learning and growth. Ruth understood that what "sounds" like criticism may be pointing toward new solutions or options. She can take this feedback on board because she has moved outside of dualistic, either/or thinking. At the same time, she is careful and effective in providing constructive feedback to others. She doesn't need to prove someone else is wrong in order to lead and can focus on information rather than ego posturing.

In fact, communication of feedback and other types of information is one of the key ingredients of conscious leadership. Effectively listening and communicating will take you a long way, and empowers others to express themselves and do their best. Conscious leaders want to know the strengths and talents of the individuals on their team, and how to best leverage those strengths and talents. Their team in turn knows they can have open conversation with their leadership, and that they have a shared commitment to the outcome.

Decision-making is a prevalent action for leaders. Conscious leaders know that no decision *is* a decision. It is very frustrating for a team when decisions are not made or when they are not clearly articulated. Conscious leaders also understand there may be a price to pay for choosing a decision. They take into account the many perspectives and options available. They discuss with their team and colleagues the ultimate goal, and how they believe the team can best achieve it, given the circumstances they are working with.

Conscious leaders are supportive of healthy lifestyles that promote the individual, which is the right thing to do and also contributes to the organization. When they walk the talk and are supportive of the workforce, they understand that this creates an environment that promotes a healthy and innovative culture. Their expectations are congruent with the culture and they are aware when they are not in line with supporting the culture.

© Rosalie Chamberlain 2015

Image 9.1. Performance Excellence Intersection©. Individual strengths and talents can lead to organizational success. Performance Excellence is a result of the intersection of inclusion, engagement, motivation and innovation.

Continual growth is an important component for conscious leadership. Leaders want to contribute and create a powerful, engaging environment, and realize that growth, both for the individual and the organization, is a natural part of that dynamic. They also know that the bottom line is important and that this is a primary focus for the organization's success.

Conscious leaders know that their people are their assets and it is with their commitment and development that together they meet the bottom line. It is not a one-person show.

For a look at how this plays out in the real world, check out Great Place to Work® Best Companies to Work For lists, "the most definitive employer-of-choice and workplace culture quality recognition a company can receive." Their model "defines how relationships between employees and managers play out in five dimensions: Credibility, Respect, Fairness, Pride and Camaraderie."[7] It takes conscious leaders to support creating and sustaining an environment that enables an organization to make this list. How many of these qualities are part of your organization? Which ones would you like to add?

Summary

If you've been reading this book with its emphasis on the individual journey—how each person must ultimately claim their power for themselves—you may be wondering where that puts you as a leader of other people. Don't those you lead each have to make their own

---

7   Great Place to Work. "Identifying Best Places to Work: US and
     Globally."

journey, just as you must make yours? But then how are you to connect what they do with the larger goals of the organization, the family or the group?

Simple: by taking the steps to a more conscious awareness of your leadership, you are creating space for everyone around you to do the same. They are empowered to contribute to the overall goals. The most conscious leaders I know are eager to learn how they can be better leaders and they invite the talent and skills of the individuals they lead. They empower and tirelessly work toward creating an inclusive environment. Like Robert, they know it is the small gestures such as stopping to engage in chit-chat to connect with someone, knowing their names and looking them in the eye. He is fully present. In both Ruth's and Robert's organizations, they offer town hall meetings to invite open communication and they really enjoy being amongst their workforce. It is having an open door policy and knowing how to balance the openness with busy schedules and deadlines. Robert notes that engaging others helps overcome any perceived distance that may exist between the leader's position and their staff. The leaders I have worked with are committed to really listen and want to understand the thoughts and perspectives of those around them and the people they lead.

Robert believes it is about being genuine, authentic. It is doing what you expect others to do. If you expect them to work hard, then you are working hard as well. Conscious leaders demand more of themselves than they do of others because they are always working toward improvement and self-growth. In this way, they are role models and their team will want to follow their leadership. Your actions will speak louder than words, so it is important to lead by example and be a role model. It is walking the talk and not just checking the box on leadership skills. When this happens, people want to follow you.

By setting aside the little ego and its dualistic toys, you model for others an acceptable way for generating new ideas and productive outcomes. By identifying your triggers and your unconscious biases, you give yourself the opportunity to make thoughtful and considered decisions that will benefit your colleagues. When you end the blame game, others cease to play as well. Remember that blame begins with believing someone or something did "this." Any message of blame is disempowering. In the moment of blame, you give away your power to make change and to achieve a better outcome.

One other thing about blame is that we often blame ourselves. This is not the same as taking responsibility and making different choices once we have learned from something that did not turn out the way we wanted it to. Blaming yourself is not helpful. You get too caught up in the "shoulds" and precious energy is wasted when it could be tapping into creativity, collaboration and powerful new directions and outcomes.

When you recognize the role of fear and decide to claim your authentic power, you have already taken the first steps toward making a difference—one person at a time.

Conscious leadership begins with a single person. That person is you.

—— **Exercise** ——

1. Ask yourself if you would confidently follow your leadership? If yes, congratulations! If there is a sense of "most of the time," then explore the times you would not want to follow you. Why? What would you change?

2. Establish a "Should" Meter (an indicator of how often you tell yourself what you "should" do or be), and then check it out every time you "hear" a Should in your inner messaging. Shoulds are driven by some type of message. Once you realize the Should message, you have the opportunity to determine what your choices are; what you really want to do; what is in alignment with your values and with the organizational goals. Now you can make the choice that you feel confident about. When you pause and check out choices, you have the opportunity to choose a belief and action that is conscious. Even if there is uncertainty as to how a choice will be received, you can recognize the fear, evaluate the concerns and choose the best action. If the ego, that little ego, is not hanging on, you will be able to lower the number of Shoulds on your "Should" Meter. Make them a part of a "Confidence/Success" Meter instead.

3. Value the many perspectives you have invited to be shared from those you lead. Remember that perspectives are filters that are applied through learning and experience and since we all have our own unique background, let alone our unique talents and skills, perspectives can be rich. When

the little ego is not present, perspectives are not threatening and they provide an opportunity to grow ideas into greater ideas, products, solutions and outcomes.

4. Express gratitude. This starts with recognizing what you have to be grateful for. Express it. Another interesting daily meditation is to say 10 things you are grateful for everyday. Just allow what wants to bubble up to rise to the surface and see how easy it is to find gratitude for very small things— even things that did not go the way we planned, because we can be grateful for the learning experience. I find that when I do the 10 points of gratitude meditation, I often cannot stop at 10.

5. Redefine what you may have once called a challenge as an opportunity. It is an opportunity to think critically, engage others for collaboration, and create powerful outcomes.

ABOUT THE AUTHOR

Rosalie Chamberlain is the Owner of *Rosalie Chamberlain Consulting & Coaching*. She is a skilled consultant, facilitator, coach and speaker in the areas of diversity and inclusion strategy, multicultural competency, leadership development, talent management, with expertise in managing and leveraging diverse talent. She coaches executives and high potential professionals who are committed to taking charge of their careers. She is passionate about her work because of her commitment to helping individuals and organizations to be their best. She has 15+ years of experience coaching individuals and teams, both inside and outside of corporate environments. Her coaching style helps to identify behaviors that motivate, inspire and create, as well as those that block creativity and performance.

Rosalie's work includes strategies and programs on conscious leadership, conflict resolution, effective communication, team dynamics, cross cultural dynamics, team effectiveness, taking charge of your career and navigating through corporate culture.

She is a speaker and a facilitator of programs on Diversity and Inclusion Awareness, Exploring and Understanding Unconscious Bias, Generational Diversity, Effective Feedback, Understanding People with Disabilities and Roosevelt Thomas Consulting & Training's Diversity Skills Management. In addition to coaching one-on-one with individuals, Rosalie assists organizations in assessing their current state and helps develop actions to move the organization forward to reach desired goals.

Rosalie has spoken at national, local and regional conferences and conventions. She works with a range of national and international clients in the legal, corporate, governmental and private industries.

She is a Certified Professional Coach through iPEC (Institute for Professional Excellence in Coaching) and a certified Energy Leadership Index Practitioner, and is certified through the International Coaching Federation; a certified Neuro-Linguistic Programming (NLP) Master Practitioner; and holds certifications for Myers Briggs and Taylor Protocols Core Values Index.

Rosalie is a Cornell University ILR Certified Diversity Professional Advanced Practitioner (CCDP/AP). She is a member of The Society for Human Resource Management (SHRM), a member of the Colorado Women's Chamber of Commerce, the Denver Metro Chamber of Commerce, and is a supporter of the Center for Legal Inclusiveness. She has served as board member on both non-profit and association boards.

Rosalie is originally from Atlanta, Georgia and currently lives in Denver, Colorado.

To find out more about Rosalie, her services and work with individuals and organizations, visit her website at www.rosaliechamberlainconsulting.com.

APPENDIX: EXERCISES

Exercise 1—Who are You?

It is helpful to discover, define and write down our goals and desired outcomes with respect to becoming self-aware. These can form your roadmap toward success and you can add to it or take away from it from time to time. The important thing is that you begin to see what it is *you* really want.

1. Recognize who and where you are in the present.
2. Do you give the best toward the common goal? If not, why?
3. What price are you willing to pay to achieve your desired goal?

On a scale of 1-10, rate yourself with regard to your level of commitment to give your best. If you are not at a 10, what would it take to move up the scale? What is one action you can take to move forward in that direction?

Exercise 2—Fear

Think of a time when you were successful in moving through fear because you were confident in your abilities in that situation. Then, uncertainty or fear began tugging at you because the situation may have become more challenging or more of a risk. Remember how you moved right through the fear because your confidence and certainty kicked in.

1. How did you step outside the F.E.A.R.© cycle?
2. What questions did you ask yourself? Or, what statements did you tell yourself?
3. What conclusions did you reach that allowed you to move forward?
4. What awareness from that situation that helped you through the challenge can be available for future challenges?

Exercise 3—Bias

Begin to notice where you have judgment, fear and withholding in a situation or around some individuals. Notice judgments that pop into your head and what the messages are.

1. What assumptions are you making?
2. How might you be stereotyping an individual into a particular group?
3. Explore the early messages that influenced your perception about the particular topic.
4. What was the message and how did it impact you?
5. Are you resistant to certain subjects or aspects of diversity and inclusion? What are they?
6. Where did they come from?
7. How true are the assumptions and judgments you made? How can you influence change in future circumstances by being aware of your bias?

Experiment: Establish a Judgment Journal and note in the journal the judgments you make about others and about yourself, and see how fast it fills up.

Exercise 4—Triggers

1. Identify a challenge you see and experience in your world.
2. What are the perspectives that are learned and the ones that are habitual? List these.
3. List alternative perspectives to approach the perceived challenge. Once you examine other perspectives, what might be another way of looking at the challenge or situation?

Exercise 5—Duality

1. Listen to your either/or thinking.
   a. How do you recognize duality at work in your thoughts?
2. Listen for the one versus the other thinking.
   a. Notice if there is tension, anxiety or resistance to other perspectives and suggestions.
   b. Explore why this might be.
   c. Do you fear or believe in a negative outcome as a result of a different perspective or suggestion?
   d. Allow yourself to consider a neutral possibility.
3. Take the process deeper by discovering if there is a fear or belief of a negative outcome based on if your preferred way is not chosen.
4. Explore a middle ground.
   a. What if it is neither good nor bad, and it is just different—different from your usual way of being or doing?
5. While observing your either/or thinking, be aware if you are focusing on having a dialogue or a debate.
   a. In dialogue, you are interested in what the other has to say and they are interested in what you have to say. In a debate, it is a clear intention of either/or, right/wrong—that focuses on win/lose.
   b. How often do you have a dialogue, and how often do you have a debate?

    c.   Can you think of a situation where dialogue would be the most useful type of communication?

Exercise 6—Ego

Take another look at the Energetic Self Perception Chart developed by Bruce D Schneider (page 60). Which level best describes how you see the world? To find out exactly how your energy is distributed among the seven levels, you can deepen the exercise by arranging to take the Energy Leader Assessment to focus on shifting your consciousness and increasing your awareness, energy and leadership capabilities. Contact information for the assessment is found in the About the Author section of this book.

Exercise 7—Blame

1.   See if you can give yourself some space and time to consider negative judgments that come up.
2.   Where do these really come from?
3.   Are they based in truth?
4.   Are they habitual thoughts?

Try really listening to the message. It probably was originally intended to protect you in some form or fashion, but it now only takes away your energy, confidence and power. The deeper you go in understanding the message and the impact it has on you, the easier it will be to determine where it came from, if it is true for you and if you want to commit to let it go. If you find that there is a struggle to move out of the old message because it is all you have ever known, it can feel like being "stuck in quicksand."

If you find yourself stepping into this "quicksand," there is another step to the exercise to begin to shift the habitual message.

5. To take the process deeper, when you hear a judgment, recognize it. *But don't judge yourself or it!*

   a. Clearly identify what the judgment is and what the belief is.

   b. Now, take a moment to choose a situation when you were successful. Take time to envision the occasion in cinematic detail. Bring it fully conscious. What did it look like? Who else was there? How did they respond? How did you feel? Really embody it.

   c. What about you made it successful? *Take time with this one.* List out at least five ways you led to this success. Where can you utilize these five things in other situations? Notice you might be saying, "Now *what* was that judgment I had?" Once it has shifted, the particular self-judgment can really become a thing of the past.

   d. Afterwards, go back to that negative voice, thank it for sharing and continue looking at the qualities that you had and still have for creating another successful outcome.

Exercise 8—Authentic Power

An important aspect of claiming your authenticity is fully assessing what is important and how well you are aligned with your whole self. The following questions and exercises are important tools for creating alignment.

1. Write down your values, as many as you feel are important to you. Then narrow the list to the top five things. Where does each value currently show up in your day-to-day life? If there are any that sit in the shadows that you would like to bring more front and center, which one(s)? Why is it not a primary contributor? How can it be made into a primary contributor?

2. On a scale of 1-10, one being lowest and ten being the highest, how integrated is your mind, body and spirit? Now, spirit can mean various things to different people. It is not necessarily religious, as it can be intuition, wisdom, higher self, divine—however you define it for you. There will be times when we utilize one aspect more than another, and at the same time, the other two are still a part of who we are. What does the integration of your mind, body and spirit look or feel like for you? Begin to notice these three aspects and how they interrelate in your day-to-day activities. Ignoring one or more parts can ultimately lead to imbalance. The Aristotle quote, "*The whole is greater than the sum of its parts,*" can be a

guiding statement to maintaining a balance of mind, body and spirit.

3. Consider a meditative practice as a regular part of your daily life. Whether it is a walk outside, a calm quiet time set aside, reading something that is empowering and motivating—it does not matter. Just focus on whatever gives you that sense of being calm and connected, free of worry or fear, and fully present. Find ways to make this an important part of your life—just like eating and sleeping and brushing your teeth. After a while, you will be compelled to do it. There are many books on meditative and mindful practices. A couple I recommend are *Search Inside Yourself: The Unexpected Path to Achieving Success, Happiness (and World Peace)*, by Chade-Meng Tan, and *Mindfulness: An Eight-Week Plan for Finding Peace in a Frantic World*, by Mark Williams and Danny Penman.

4. What gives you joy? What energizes you? How much of that energizing factor do you have in your life and work? How can you have more?

5. If you were to give a TED Talk, what message would you give? Once you have determined your message, assess whether it is a part of how you show up in your work and in your life.

6. What "stories" have you invested in about yourself? How have they worked for you? Do they align with your values? If not, how would you rewrite your story to be authentically you?

Exercise 9—Confidently Lead

1. Ask yourself if you would confidently follow your leadership? If yes, congratulations! If there is a sense of "most of the time," then explore the times you would not want to follow you. Why? What would you change?

2. Establish a "Should" Meter (an indicator of how often you tell yourself what you "should" do or be), and then check it out every time you "hear" a Should in your inner messaging. Shoulds are driven by some type of message. Once you realize the Should message, you have the opportunity to determine what your choices are; what you really want to do; what is in alignment with your values and with the organizational goals. Now you can make the choice that you feel confident about. When you pause and check out choices, you have the opportunity to choose a belief and action that is conscious. Even if there is uncertainty as to how a choice will be received, you can recognize the fear, evaluate the concerns and choose the best action. If the ego, that little ego, is not hanging on, you will be able to lower the number of Shoulds on your "Should" Meter. Make them a part of a "Confidence/Success" Meter instead.

3. Value the many perspectives you have invited to be shared from those you lead. Remember that perspectives are filters that are applied through learning and experience and since we all have our own unique background, let alone our unique talents and skills, perspectives can be rich. When the

little ego is not present, perspectives are not threatening and they provide an opportunity to grow ideas into greater ideas, products, solutions and outcomes.

4. Express gratitude. This starts with recognizing what you have to be grateful for. Express it. Another interesting daily meditation is to say 10 things you are grateful for everyday. Just allow what wants to bubble up to rise to the surface and see how easy it is to find gratitude for very small things— even things that did not go the way we planned, because we can be grateful for the learning experience. I find that when I do the 10 points of gratitude meditation, I often cannot stop at 10.

5. Redefine what you may have once called a challenge as an opportunity. It is an opportunity to think critically, engage others for collaboration, and create powerful outcomes.

NOTES

Introduction:
Goleman, Daniel. *Emotional Intelligence: Why It Can Matter More than IQ.* Bantam, 1995.

Chapter 1:
Prive, Tanye. "Top 10 Qualities that Make a Great Leader." *Forbes.* Published online December 19, 2012.

Chapter 2:
Gregoire, Carolyn. "The Science of Conquering Your Fears—and Living a More Courageous Life." *The Huffington Post.* Published online September 15, 2013.

Brown, PhD, Brené. *Daring Greatly: How the Courage to Be Vulnerable Transforms the Way We Live, Love, Parent, and Lead.* Avery, 2015.

Chapter 3:

Johns, PhD, RHIA, Merida L. "Breaking the Glass Ceiling: Structural, Cultural, and Organizational Barriers Preventing Women from Achieving Senior and Executive Positions." *Perspectives in Health Information Management.*

Warner, Judith. "Fact Sheet: The Women's Leadership Gap, Women's Leadership by the Numbers" *Center for American Progress.*

Catalyst. *Narrowing the Fortune 100 Gender Leadership Gap: Change is Closer Than You Think.* 2012.

Chapter 9:

Great Place to Work. "Identifying Best Places to Work: US and Globally."

REFERENCES

Brown, PhD, Brené. *Daring Greatly: How the Courage to Be Vulnerable Transforms the Way We Live, Love, Parent, and Lead.* Avery, 2015.

Catalyst. *Narrowing the Fortune 100 Gender Leadership Gap: Change is Closer Than You Think.* 2012.

Goleman, Daniel. *Emotional Intelligence: Why It Can Matter More than IQ.* Bantam, 1995.

Great Place to Work. "Identifying Best Places to Work: US and Globally."

Gregoire, Carolyn. "The Science of Conquering Your Fears – and Living a More Courageous Life." *The Huffington Post.* Published online September 15, 2013.

Johns, PhD, RHIA, Merida L. "Breaking the Glass Ceiling: Structural, Cultural, and Organizational Barriers Preventing Women from Achieving Senior and Executive Positions." *Perspectives in Health Information Management.*

Prive, Tanye. "Top 10 Qualities that Make a Great Leader." *Forbes.* Published online December 19, 2012.

Reeves, Dr. Arin. *The Next IQ: The Next Level of Intelligence for 21st Century Leaders.* American Bar Association, 2012.

Schneider, Bruce D *Energy Leadership: Transforming Your Workplace and Your Life from the Core.* John Wiley & Sons, Inc., 2007.

Warner, Judith. "Fact Sheet: The Women's Leadership Gap, Women's Leadership by the Numbers" *Center for American Progress.*

RESOURCES

To further explore the concepts and practices I have discussed in this book, see suggestions for additional reading below:

Page, Scott E. *The Difference: How the Power of Diversity Creates Better Groups, Firms, Schools, and Societies*. Princeton University Press, 2007.

Reeves, Dr. Arin. "Written in Black & White: Exploring Confirmation Bias in Racialized Perceptions of Writing Skills." *Nextions Yellow Paper Series*.

Minority Corporate Counsel Association (MCCA).

Interesting books on meditative and mindful practices include:

    Search Inside Yourself: The Unexpected Path to Achieving Success, Happiness (and World Peace), by Chade-Meng Tan (HarperOne,

2012), and *Mindfulness: An Eight-Week Plan for Finding Peace in a Frantic World*, by Mark Williams and Danny Penman (Rodale, 2011).